Chart Hits

CONTENTS

2   All About That Bass MEGHAN TRAINOR

4   All of Me JOHN LEGEND

6   Happy PHARRELL WILLIAMS

8   Radioactive IMAGINE DRAGONS

10 Roar KATY PERRY

12 Say Something A GREAT BIG WORLD

16 Shake It Off TAYLOR SWIFT

18 A Sky Full of Stars COLDPLAY

13 Someone Like You ADELE

24 Stay with Me SAM SMITH

20 Thinking Out Loud ED SHEERAN

22 Uptown Funk MARK RONSON FEATURING BRUNO MARS

To access audio visit:
www.halleonard.com/mylibrary

Enter Code
7005-2787-6332-6766

Audio Arrangements by Peter Deneff

ISBN 978-1-4950-2305-7

HAL•LEONARD®
CORPORATION

7777 W. BLUEMOUND RD. P.O. BOX 13819 MILWAUKEE, WI 53213

Visit Hal Leonard Online at
www.halleonard.com

ALL ABOUT THAT BASS

HORN

Words and Music by KEVIN KADISH
and MEGHAN TRAINOR

ALL OF ME

HORN

Words and Music by JOHN STEPHENS
and TOBY GAD

HAPPY
from DESPICABLE ME 2

HORN

Words and Music by
PHARRELL WILLIAMS

RADIOACTIVE

Horn

Words and Music by DANIEL REYNOLDS,
BENJAMIN McKEE, DANIEL SERMON,
ALEXANDER GRANT and JOSH MOSSER

ROAR

Horn

Words and Music by KATY PERRY,
LUKASZ GOTTWALD, MAX MARTIN,
BONNIE McKEE and HENRY WALTER

SAY SOMETHING

Horn

Words and Music by IAN AXEL,
CHAD VACCARINO and MIKE CAMPBELL

SOMEONE LIKE YOU

Horn

Words and Music by ADELE ADKINS
and DAN WILSON

SHAKE IT OFF

Horn

Words and Music by TAYLOR SWIFT,
MAX MARTIN and SHELLBACK

A SKY FULL OF STARS

HORN

Words and Music by GUY BERRYMAN,
JON BUCKLAND, WILL CHAMPION,
CHRIS MARTIN and TIM BERGLING

THINKING OUT LOUD

HORN

Words and Music by ED SHEERAN
and AMY WADGE

UPTOWN FUNK

Horn

Words and Music by MARK RONSON,
BRUNO MARS, PHILIP LAWRENCE,
JEFF BHASKER, DEVON GALLASPY
and NICHOLAUS WILLIAMS

STAY WITH ME

Horn

Words and Music by SAM SMITH,
JAMES NAPIER and WILLIAM EDWARD PHILLIPS